Barry Rowe

GRAND PRIX

The know-how of racing and racing cars

COLLINS COLOUR CUBS

Grand Prix motor racing, the most glamorous and dangerous sport of them all, began in 1906. The French Grand Prix came first and was run over a course of 769 miles, the winner's average speed being 63 miles per hour. The horrible state of the roads at that time made sure that the mechanic who sat beside the driver was not just along for the ride.

For nearly half a century, the Grand Prix scene was dominated by front-engined cars. Then, in 1959, Cooper Cars put the engine in the back of the car and started a run of successes including the Monaco Grand Prix. All the leading designers got the message. Cars with the engine in front were out. The new designs all had the engine mounted in the rear.

Formula One is the Grand Prix formula. The International Automobile Federation lays down specifications concerning engine size, minimum weight and type of structure, body width, fuel tanks and the amount of petrol that can be carried. Formula One racing cars must also have a fire extinguishing system. The design team must bear all these specifications in mind.

Mock-up shapes of the new design are tested in a wind tunnel. Coloured tapes are stuck all over the car and observed by designers. These feed back

information which may result in the shape of the car being modified until air drag is negative.

The current Formula One engine is limited to 3,000 c.c. or 1,500, turbo-charged. The racing engine revs up to 11,500 revs per minute. Petrol consumption varies from 5.7 to 7 miles to the gallon. The life of the engine is only 1200 miles. After that, it is re-built.

Castings arrive in the machine shop from specialist manufacturers in a roughly finished state. Components like suspension units and monocoque bulkheads have to be machined.

All the holes are drilled out and polished here by specialist engineers. The wheels are also built and machined in this workshop.

In the fabricating shop, the monocoque
is built up. It consists of sheets of
aluminium cut, shaped and riveted
together. Other strong, but light, metals
such as titanium are also used. This part of
the car has to be very strong since it is the
area in which the driver sits. The rear wing is
also constructed in similar fashion.

In the glass-fibre shop, bodywork for racing cars is made. A mould is taken from a prototype body. The finished glass-fibre body is in self-coloured resin. The driver's seat is also made in this manner. Many spare bodies are made to replace parts damaged in races.

The next stage sees the fitting of all the pipes and fuel lines from the petrol tanks. The petrol carried is limited to 250 litres and the tanks must have fire-proof safety construction. The fire-extinguishing system is also fitted at this point; and the suspension mountings are bolted together.

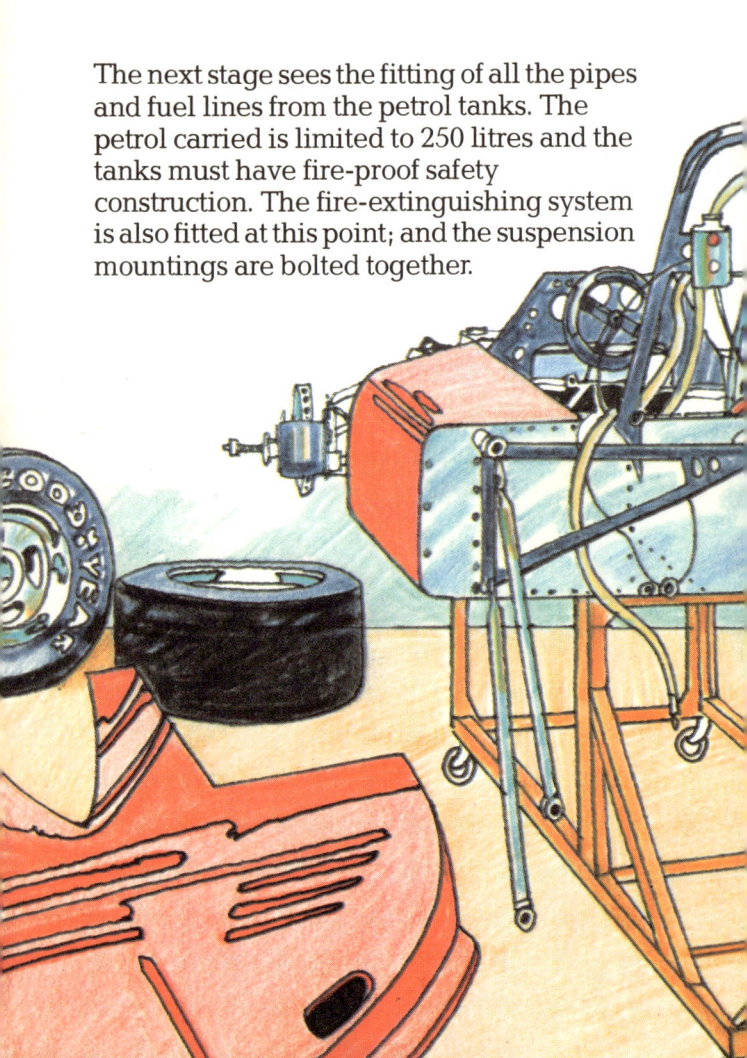

The engine and gear-box are now bolted to the monocoque. The gear-box has five gears and will last only 1200 miles between rebuilds. Two strong men can lift an engine. This is because it is constructed from magnesium, a metal that is as strong as it is light.

Next, the glass-fibre panels are fitted to the monocoque. The brakes have been bolted together, the front brakes on the wheel hubs. The rear brakes are mounted inboard. The disc-brake system, now used in practically every production car, was developed in racing cars. Tyre development has become important in recent years. Tyres are made from a special compound specially developed for racing. They are twenty inches wide and have an air pressure of ten to fourteen pounds per square inch.

Instruments tell the driver what is happening in the engine compartment.

Testing now begins. The car covers hundreds of miles at a racing circuit. Many adjustments are made to suspension and brakes. The car nose may possibly be altered to allow more ducted air to the oil cooler. Experiments are carried out with the tyres at different air pressures.

The car is now ready for action. Every Grand Prix team has a team manager who is responsible for organising the car for a race. The rest of the team consists of a chief mechanic and three mechanics for each car, and a team secretary who does all the paper work that is involved.

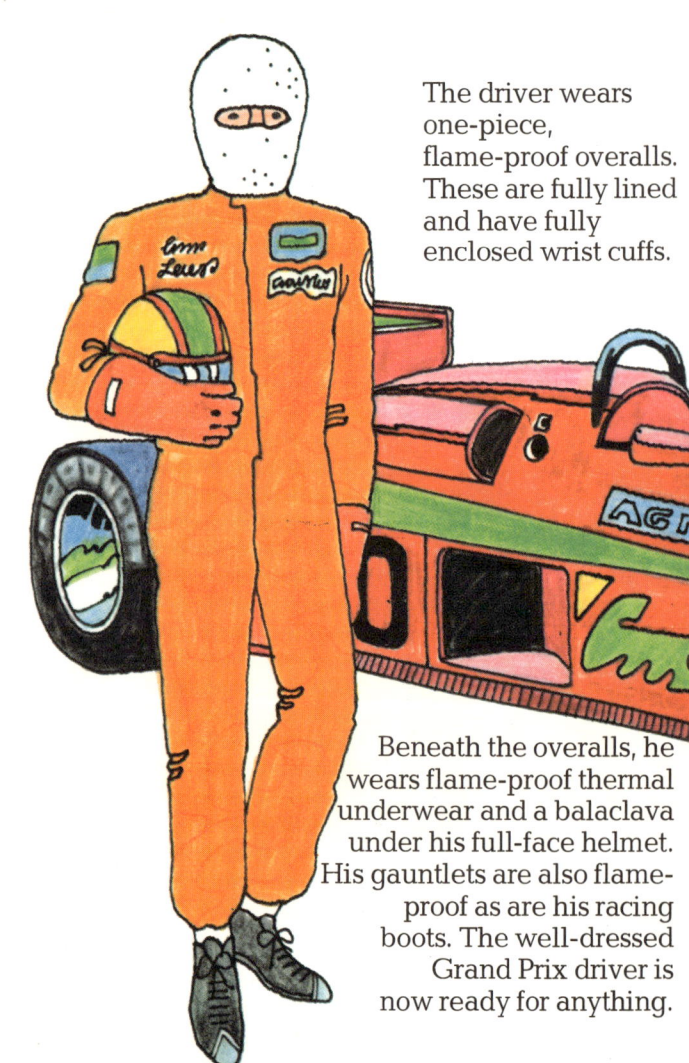

The driver wears one-piece, flame-proof overalls. These are fully lined and have fully enclosed wrist cuffs.

Beneath the overalls, he wears flame-proof thermal underwear and a balaclava under his full-face helmet. His gauntlets are also flame-proof as are his racing boots. The well-dressed Grand Prix driver is now ready for anything.

His safety helmet is fitted with a rubber tube. This supplies medical air through special ducts in the helmet. In the event of a serious accident, this medical air will prolong what may prove to be vital survival time.

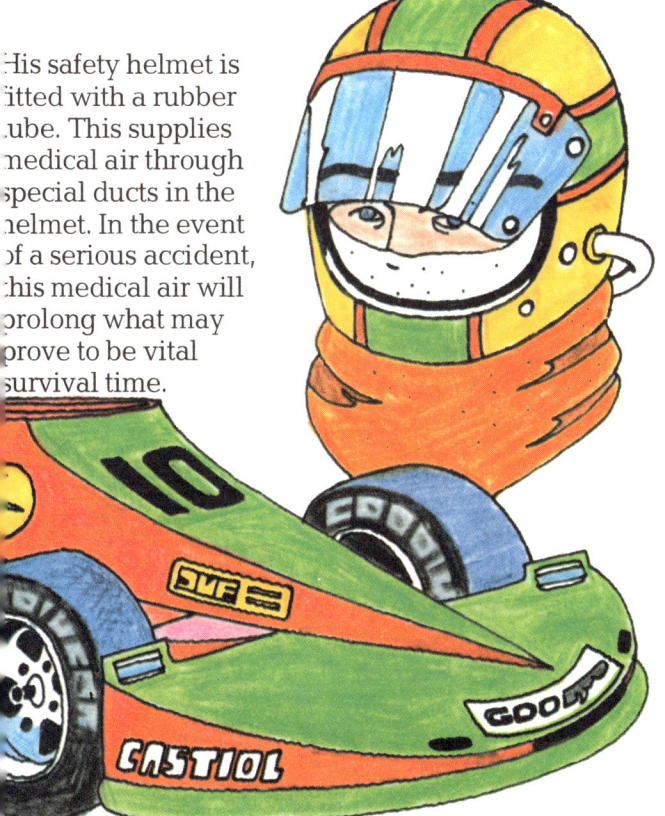

Sponsors provide vast sums of money for racing teams. In return for this, the cars carry the sponsors' names and stickers. A successful racing team has tremendous advertising value.

Grand Prix cars travel to races all over the world in special transporters. These are, in effect, travelling workshops. They carry spare engines, gear-boxes and any other spare part that may be required. In one single racing season, a transporter may cover as many as 20,000 miles.

Lots of spare tyres are needed for practice days at all the Grand Prix races.

A Grand Prix race is usually limited to
26 cars. Each car entered is rigorously
scrutinised by the race organisers'
engineers to make certain that it
complies with the rules. Before the
actual race, there are two practice days
and the fastest car has pole position on
the starting grid.

During official practice, a car can cover between 500 and 600 miles.

The marshals of the course use international flag signals. Every racing driver is required to be familiar with these.

The national flag of the host country starts the race.

Blue flag: you are being followed. Waved: you are about to be overtaken.

Red and yellow: slippery surface, oil on the track. When waved: extreme caution.

Yellow flag: caution, danger ahead. Waved: prepare to stop.

Red flag waved: all cars stop immediately. Racing terminated.

White flag: caution, service vehicle on track. Waved: service vehicle directly ahead.

Black flag: car with number shown come into pits next time round.

Chequered flag: the race winner has crossed the finishing line. The race is over.

Every ticket for a motor race bears the message: "Motor Racing is Dangerous". Every possible precaution is taken to reduce this danger. Fire marshals stand on every corner by the Armco crash barriers. Doctors and ambulances are stationed near dangerous corners. Fire-tenders, with all necessary apparatus, are positioned round the circuit.

The start of a Grand Prix race is deafening for the spectators and important for the drivers who must try to get in front on the first lap. Acceleration on these cars is fantastic. They go from 0-100 miles an hour in a mere five seconds.

If the weather changes during a race, there has to be a tyre change in the pits. Dry tyres, called "slicks" have no tread, only small slits.

Wet weather tyres have a tread but the compound wears out quickly on a dry track. If the weather changes the pit mechanics really earn their money.

The team manager and his mechanics work very hard in the pits while the drivers are jousting out on the track. Every lap is timed on stop watches and this information is relayed to the driver by means of signal boards. The driver acknowledges the message by a thumbs-up gesture.

The first car to complete the number of laps laid down by the organisers is the winner of the race. After 200 miles of split-second decisions and razor-edged racing, the chequered flag is a welcome sight. A lap of honour follows.

The winner is
presented with a trophy and a laurel wreath.
The second and third drivers are also presented
on the winner's rostrum. Championship points
are awarded: 9 points for first, 6 points for
second, 4 points for third, 2 points for fifth,
1 point for sixth.

And for the driver who sets a new
lap record: a hundred bottles of
champagne.

The driver who turns in the best six performances in the World Championship wins the title of "World Championship Driver". The Formula One Constructors Championship goes to the maker of the car. The sponsors, in turn, reap their reward. Their products enjoy enormous exposure on television and the other media for the rest of the year until along comes another World Championship, another new car, another brilliant team — and another World Champion.

TEXT BY EDWARD BOYD

Illustrations Copyright © 1978 Barry Rowe
Text Copyright © 1978 Wm. Collins Sons & Co. Ltd.
ISBN 0 00 123260 6
Printed in Great Britain